YOUR KNOWLEDGE HAS VALUE

- We will publish your bachelor's and master's thesis, essays and papers

- Your own eBook and book - sold worldwide in all relevant shops

- Earn money with each sale

Upload your text at www.GRIN.com and publish for free

Bibliographic information published by the German National Library:

The German National Library lists this publication in the National Bibliography; detailed bibliographic data are available on the Internet at http://dnb.dnb.de .

Imprint:

Copyright © 2018 GRIN Verlag
Print and binding: Books on Demand GmbH, Norderstedt Germany
ISBN: 9783346014580

This book at GRIN:

https://www.grin.com/document/498029

Eva Marx

Political Polarization in the USA and the 2016 Election

GRIN Verlag

GRIN - Your knowledge has value

Since its foundation in 1998, GRIN has specialized in publishing academic texts by students, college teachers and other academics as e-book and printed book. The website www.grin.com is an ideal platform for presenting term papers, final papers, scientific essays, dissertations and specialist books.

Visit us on the internet:

http://www.grin.com/

http://www.facebook.com/grincom

http://www.twitter.com/grin_com

It's a Movement, Not a Campaign

Political Polarization in the USA and the 2016 Election

Research Paper in Advanced English
Conrad-von-Soest-Gymnasium
By Eva Marx

Structure

1. Introduction

The election of the former businessman and TV personality Donald J. Trump as the 45th president of the United States of America (US) was a shock not only for America but also for the world. The unprecedented outcome of the election on 8th November 2016 followed a campaign like no other the world had ever seen before. Although struggling in the polls in the course of the electoral campaign, Trump managed to win 306 electoral delegates over to his side compared to his opponent Hillary Clinton's 232 electoral delegates. Because of the unpredictable result of the 2016 electoral campaign, I was highly interested in the background of and reasons for this development which I am going to elaborate in further detail.

In order to understand why such an unforeseen event as Trump winning the election could happen, it is necessary to examine the political development in recent years leading to the image of American politics that can be seen today. Moreover, one needs to consider the electoral strategy of the Trump campaign targeting the hate and distrust of parts of the American population against the Washington establishment.

Therefore, one has to ask themselves how American politics became as polarized as they are today and how Trump was able to use the polarization within the population to promote his campaign. Furthermore, it is crucial to take a look at in how far the nomination of Hillary Clinton as his opponent played into Trump's hands as well.

In the following, I am going to give a brief overview of the literature I used and some background information about the biography of Donald Trump and American politics in the past. Subsequently, I will analyse the political development that left the US as a deeply divided country in terms of political polarization as well as the strategy of Trump's campaign against all elites. Another focus of the analysis is going to be the nomination of Clinton and its consequences for the Trump campaign. Thereupon, I am going to conclude by answering my research questions and by presenting a possible prospect of the next presidential election in 2020.

2. Overview

2.1 Literature

The analysis is based on the books "Die Akte Trump" by David C. Johnston which focuses on the important events in the life of the current President, "Die gespaltenen Staaten von Amerika" by Winand Gellner and Michael Oswald consisting of essays by various authors which deal with several analyses of the election and the political polarization throughout the last decades, and "The Unprecedented 2016 Presidential Election" by Rachel Bitecofer which attempts to explain the election through a strategic focus. Another book that was used is "Nach Obama" by Christoph Bieber which emphasizes Trump's use of the political cleavage of the population, as well as numerous polls and surveys and the worksheet "Isolationism vs. Internationalism".[1]

2.2 Background Information

Biography of Donald J. Trump.[2] The Trump family first set their foot on American ground when Friedrich Trump, Donald Trump's grandfather, moved to the US to avoid serving in the German military in 1885. He then started the "family tradition" of accumulating wealth with questionable methods. After the early death of Friedrich Trump, his wife Elizabeth and his twelve-year old son Frederick founded the car park construction company Elizabeth Trump & Son, Fred's ticket into the world of the real estate industry. On his way to extreme wealth he did not hesitate to build relationships with criminals such as the Mafia families Genovese and Gambino (which "are maintained by Donald Trump decades later"). Fred later married and had five children, Donald, born on the 14th June 1946 in New York, was his fourth child. He attended an undergraduate-program at the University of Pennsylvania and acquired a bachelor in economic sciences. After his graduation, Trump took his place in his father's company and started transacting his own real estate business. He later divided his business segments into properties (e.g. golf courses), hotels, gambling and apartment buildings. In order to reach international popularity, he proceeded to build his "landmark on the Fifth Avenue, the Trump Tower". Furthermore, he is the author of several books (e.g. "The Art of the Deal"), temporarily was the owner of his private football-team and was starring in the TV series "The Apprentice". Estimating his capital is very difficult

---

[1] All quotes from German textbooks are translated by me and are not specifically accounted in the analysis.
[2] All quotes are taken from the book "Die Akte Trump".

considering his varying statements about it, however, it is publicly known that Trump was almost heading for ruin in 1990 and could only be rescued by the government since he was deemed "too big to fail". Trump married three times, the first time in 1977 Ivana Trump who bore his first three children Donald Jr., Ivanka and Eric. His second marriage to Marla Maples started in 1993 and resulted in the birth of Tiffany Trump. Currently, Donald Trump is married to Melania Trump who he had his youngest son Barron with.

Brief summary of American politics and historical events.[3] As early as the first Puritan settlements on American ground were founded, Americans had a "missionary aspiration": The Puritan preacher John Winthrop phrased it as "a shining city upon a hill", meaning that "every nation has concluded an accord with God and the Puritans had to leave England because it was breached there" so the new American community "should be a model for other countries".[4] Phases of internationalism alternated with phases of isolationism. In the first half of the 20th century the US twice decided to become involved in a world war to pave the way for democracy and later (after 1945) "fought against what they considered to be in the way of an ideal state of the world": The Soviet Union. The 1960s were an era of American over-extension of powers (especially in the Vietnam War). The next 10 years were "a decade of great reluctance in terms of US engagements" in which isolationist views gained ground. This decade was followed by "renewed international activism" in the 1980s with military interventions against communism and terrorism. After the Soviet Union had broken apart, the US was the "sole remaining global power" and although it is "trying to avoid the danger of again over-extending its powers […] it is still being constantly asked to become active in trouble spots all over the world". After the terror attack on 9/11 a new era of war against terror began under President Bush, starting the invasion of Iraq and Afghanistan with the justification of the Bush Doctrine[5].

---

[3] Unless accounted otherwise, all quotes are taken from the worksheet "Isolationism vs. Internationalism".
[4] Bieber, C., 2017, p.37
[5] Bieber, C., 2017, p. 18f

3. Analysis

3.1 America as a Divided Country

Long ago, there was a time when America had a clear conception of itself: It wanted to be the model-community for other nations to follow which can be seen "at different times, for example during the Cold War and recently in the war against terrorism"[6]. Another deeply American image is the American Dream, a common theme meaning that everyone, no matter the birth, gender, ancestry or ethnicity could pursue any career they wanted ("From rags to riches"). This illustrates some of the American values such as freedom, equal opportunities, self-responsibility and individualism[7]. During the post-war era, the American Exceptionalism (the concept that the US was protected from political disasters by God himself) gained popularity within the population. However, these ingrained values are heavily questioned by parts of the American population: The so-called "working poor [...] who quite contrary to the American Dream work hard all their life without gaining promotion"[8]. Referring to a 2014 survey by CNN, two thirds of the respondents thought that their children would have a worse life than themselves and 59% were of the opinion that it was impossible to live the American Dream by now[9].

But not only the American values have changed during the last century: Also, the relationship between the population and politicians has been deteriorating. This development was caused by several lies politicians told, e.g. the Tonkin incident during the Vietnam war or the Watergate scandal, John F. Kennedy finding a missile gap without it being there (and he knew it) and Bill Clinton in the Lewinsky affair[10]. More recently, the tissue of lies about the allegation of the possession of weapons of mass destruction leading to the Iraq war under President Bush in 2002 and the thorough staged termination of said war could be named[11].

Apart from these political scandals, the population has had another crisis of confidence concerning their own politicians: Many Americans do not feel represented in current politics anymore. Referring to data of the PEW Research Center, about 70% of the respondents had trust in their government during the 1960s, while only about 20%

---

[6] Bieber, C., 2017, p. 37
[7] Bieber, C., 2017, p. 38f
[8] Bieber, C., 2017, p. 39
[9] CNN Survey „The American Dream is out of reach"
[10] Bieber, C., 2017, p. 113
[11] Bieber, C., 2017, p. 20

reported having trust in their politicians in a recent survey in 2015[12]. This relates to the fact that the US has been pursuing a policy of "aiding the rich while forgetting about the middle class". The same survey from 2015 also discovered that two thirds of the respondents agreed on the statement the government was only there for the interests of some, and 77% thought that the elites in Washington lost contact to the average population.

Another correlation can be established between the loss of trust and the rising income disparity. In the US like in many other countries, the gap between rich and poor has been growing:

> "The top 1% of the income distribution could achieve a growth of 275% [between 1979 and 2007], whereas the wage of the middle-class workers grew at a rate of 40%. The payment of the lowest 20% of the income distribution only increased by 18%".

What is different in comparison to other countries is the rate at which the US government is interfering with the redistribution of taxes. It turns out here that the "redistribution of taxes and social transfers in the US are at a remarkable lower level than in many other developed democracies" and they decreased even more during the 1990s and at the beginning of the century. "In addition, the finance, economy and real estate crisis [in 2008] aggravated the situation". Other problems are the technological development, long-term unemployment and a declining level of employment overall[13].

All of this in combination with the Civil Rights Act, the Voting Rights Act and other movements such as the women's liberation movement led to a cultural revolution taking place since the 1960s[14]. "It provoked a lasting alienation from the ideal of a plural but jointly acting nation ("e pluribus unum") mostly in conservative groups" who felt like minorities of any kind determined the core of the political life[15]. These changes caused a "culture-war" in which the Republican and Democratic parties came to symbolize opposing fractions – "Once ideologically diverse, the parties had sorted into ideologically homogenous camps: Liberals into the Democratic Party and conservatives into the Republican Party". Eventually, the number of ideologically moderate members in both parties decreased dramatically[16]. Furthermore, the outer bonds of the ideological

---

[12] PEW Research Center Survey „Beyond Distrust: How Americans View Their Government"
[13] Gellner, W.; Oswald, M., 2018, p. 212-218
[14] Bitecofer, R., 2017, p. 12
[15] Gellner, W.; Oswald, M., 2018, p. V
[16] Bitecofer, R., 2017, p. 13f

spectrum stretched as a consequence of the homogeneity within campaign elites as well as their parties' voters, leading to "an increase of ideological extremism"[17].

This also explains why the level of polarization rose as much during the last eight years – the term of office of America's first Afro-American president Barack Obama who was seen as the impersonation of minorities infiltrating politics by some political extremists. His aim to unite the nation as one was destined to fail: Only weeks into his presidency, the protest movement tea party (tea as an acronym of Taxed Enough Already) was founded and resulted in demonstrations against the policies of Obama[18]. The Tea Party movement eventually gained ground in the senate and in the House of Representatives, causing a shift to the right within the party. This progress can be illustrated by a long-term study carried out by the Manifesto Project: Whereas the period shortly after the turn of the millennium was characterized as "moderately polarized", 2012 marked a rise of differences[19].

3.2 Campaign Against All Elites

The Trump campaign was quick to use these shifts within the population for their own purpose. As early as the primaries he decided to pursue a strategy of "[tapping] into the growing populist, anti-establishment sentiment within the Republican base that first emerged with the rise of the Tea Party in 2010". He also turned his back towards traditional Republican Party positions concerning economy, allowing him to cast his mainstream Republican rivals as "elites" and "insiders" bent on maintaining their economic domination over regular Americans[20].

However, most importantly he painted a gloomy picture of life in the US today – decline, failed government and danger, "the integrity of society and its organic structure violated [by the] ruling elite"[21], in other words by the Democrats. In his speeches, Trump makes use of

> "three dimensions of time and divides the future's one into two different alternatives: 1. The US has had a golden age. 2. The country is currently dilapidated. 3. The future could 3.1 either be a prospering development like the one in [the nation's] past; 3.2 or end in even greater disaster".[22]

---

[17] Bitecofer, R., 2017, p. 15f
[18] Bieber, C., 2017, p. 25
[19] Survey "Manifesto Project"
[20] Bitecofer, R., 2017, p. 40
[21] Gellner, W.; Oswald, M., 2018, p. 154
[22] Gellner, W.; Oswald, M., 2018, p. 142

Trump divided the nation's prospects into the utopian one (cf. point 3.1) in case he was going to be elected and a dystopian one (cf. point 3.2) in case his opponent Hillary Clinton was going to be elected. The central point he wanted to make was that only he was able to establish a basis for the resurgence of the US. Nevertheless, it can be noted that "it remains unclear which new system, which methods could bring improvement"[23].

It is striking that Trump utilizes nostalgia as a form of rhetorical device while giving speeches. The reason standing behind it is simply that nostalgia can be seen as a form of emotion: It can "create mental images and ideas of times when life was good". Withal, these imaginations do not have to relate to a past that actually existed this way; They can "create the impression [within the recipient] that they have been removed from the ideal of their memories provoking feelings of grief and loss" anyway. Even his slogan "Make America Great Again" perfectly fits into this theme. Nostalgia is a vitally important tool in times of cultural changes, "arising directly from the feeling of a decline of the culture". It can be seen as an escape into the past, creating a longing for former conditions. Nostalgia and a fear of deteriorating living conditions tend to go hand in hand. Nostalgia as a rhetorical device is used in populist approaches often and targets discrepancies between government and population. It is often paired up with traditionalism to fuel fears of the future[24].

The use of this type of rhetorical device can possibly lead to a felt connection between the speaker and the audience ("In-Group cohesion"). It conveys a feeling of a "common destiny" and creates a "shared identity". Such an In-Group cohesion can be formed by generating anxiety about an 'internal enemy' – "The own group and their identity is outlined as the victim of a malicious elite. […] Society is divided in a clash between the 'virtuous people' and the 'harmful elite'". By the use of nostalgia as a stylistic device, the necessity of comprehensive measures and a strong leadership - as offered by Trump himself - is emphasized on the one hand, on the other hand established standards (e.g. tolerance and multiculturalism) are discredited[25].

In addition to this strategy, Trump also had an astonishing approach towards media. Whereas other candidates payed millions for their advertising spots and presence in the media, Trump planned his campaign around relying on his celebrity status and causing controversy in order to dominate the news cycle. He pursued a strategy of "media

---

[23] Bieber, C., 2017, p. 125
[24] Gellner, W.; Oswald, M., 2018, p. 144-146
[25] Gellner, W.; Oswald, M., 2018, p. 146f

dominance via controversy" which allowed him to keep the conversation focused only on his own candidacy while concurrently depriving his political rivals of media attention for themselves[26]. This kind of media coverage is known as Free Media since the candidate does neither initiate nor pay for the reporting. According to a The New York Times analysis, as of March 15, 2016, Trump amassed at least $2 million US dollars of free media coverage, translating into over 1000 hours of reporting he did not have to pay for. The first Republican debate became the most watched non-sports cable program ever (more than 24 million viewers) and nearly 84 million viewers watched the first debate between Trump and Clinton, the most-watched debate in American history. Days of high media coverage coincide with some of Trump's most controversial moments[27]. During those periods in which Trump frequently appeared in the media, he also underwent a rise in the polls. However,

> "by tapping into the Republican electorate's distrust of the mainstream media, Trump was able to discredit them and neutralize any damage that might have resulted from some of his more outlandish behaviors among the Republican base"[28].

3.3 Clinton as Trump's Political Opponent

2016 was a hard year for the American electorate since they quite literally had to decide between bad and worse. According to Gallup, Donald Trump and Hillary Clinton are the two most disliked presidential nominees in history. Clinton ended the election with an unfavourable rating of 52%, Trump's unfavourable rating even accounted for 61%. During the 120 days of the general election neither Clinton nor Trump spent a single day positive in their net favourability[29]. In order to illustrate the voters' impression of the candidates, Bitecofer carried out a survey analysing how the respondents evaluated the presidential nominees in terms of their qualification for office. Participants were asked for the first word that comes to mind when thinking about Trump as well as Clinton. These words were later arranged in word clouds, the size of the font dependent on the frequency of the word.

---

[26] Bitecofer, R., 2017, p. 41
[27] Bitecofer, R., 2017, p. 46-48
[28] Bitecofer, R., 2017, p. 42
[29] Gallup Survey „Trump and Clinton Finish with Historically Poor Images"

| Fig. 1 Hillary Clinton word cloud | Fig. 2 Donald Trump word cloud |

The result underlines "that many voters felt they faced a choice between voting for a well-qualified liar and voting for a crazy, perhaps even racist, idiot"[30].

The Clinton team knew that their candidate suffered from serious issues resulting from her image as the "prototype of a member of the suspiciously observed Washington establishment"[31]. "Since the inauguration of Bill Clinton in 1992, a continually growing distrust in the political elite can be noted" and Hillary Clinton, wife of Bill Clinton, ex-senator of New York and former foreign minister, will always be seen as part of this establishment[32]. Therefore, one of her biggest mistakes was to make the contrast between her own political professionality and Trump's strangely amateurish behaviour a subject of discussion since that was understood as a sort of "the Washington establishment's desperate defensive reflexes"[33]. Despite the fact that their candidate was only slightly less disliked than Donald Trump, the Clinton team did almost nothing to address her public image issues; Instead, "they ignored it until the final weeks of the general election"[34].

However, this was not the only fault made by the Clinton campaign. As part of both presidential nominees' strategies, her campaign events mainly limited to the six "swing states": Florida, North Carolina, Pennsylvania, Ohio, Virginia and Michigan. 94% of all events took place in 12 different states and there were still 25 states that have not been rewarded with a visit by either of the candidates. This circumstance arises from the American voting procedure of the Electoral College: Most states are "impregnable base stations of either of the parties [red or blue states]" which traditionally results in the focus on the remaining battleground ones. Eventually, this results in a "locally 'twisted' political socialisation" in the so-called forgotten states which are only side stages of the

---

[30] Bitecofer, R., 2017, p. 95
[31] Bieber, C., 2017, p. 8
[32] Bieber, C., 2017, p. 118f
[33] Bieber, C., 2017, p. 104
[34] Bitecofer, R., 2017, p. 134

electoral campaigns[35]. The political information intake transforms into a sort of media diet which paves the way for populist messages such as the ones in the Trump campaign. Overall, Clinton hosted way less events (47 rallies between August 1st and Election Day in comparison to 120 events hosted by Trump) and chose slightly different states. "While Clinton's visits clustered almost entirely in the [...] swing states, the Trump campaign sent their candidate to a broader array of states including safe Republican states"[36]. It should be noted that, even though frequent visits do not guarantee a successful election, especially the states that Trump payed a visit to more often were the ones sealing the country's fate on election day.

Another factor that played into Donald Trump's hands well were the email-affairs haunting his competitor Hillary Clinton. The first one surfaced when Clinton was caught having sent more than 60.000 mails from a private server during her office as the foreign minister which clearly was a breach of security. The FBI started investigating against her but gave up the investigation shortly after. However, the damage had already been done: Clinton gave a press conference immediately after the report of her offence stating that she did nothing wrong. This is a lie that was not forgotten by the electorate and allowed Donald Trump to resurge his accusations against her being a "notorious liar" ("Crooked Hillary!")[37]. As time passed, the email-affair largely faded into the background until on Friday, 21st October, the FBI's Director James Comey informed the Congress about additional emails that had been revealed. Trump used the final two weeks to remind the voters of the picture he drew of Clinton as a person who "recklessly disregards national security standards". The revelation did not move Clinton voters away from her; Nevertheless, it pulled Independent voters towards voting for Trump. Three days before the election, the Congress was informed that no relevant information was contained in the mails and the investigation was closed a second time[38]. As it would be uncovered later, the FBI was "actively investigating the Trump campaign for possible collusion with the Russian government in relation to their sabotage efforts against [Clinton]"[39] – this information was, unlike the one concerning the renewed accusations against Hillary Clinton, not made public by Comey. Even if the email-affair did not directly lead to her loss, it was one of the major factors causing the election result.

---

[35] Bieber, C., 2017, p. 142f, 145
[36] Bitecofer, R., 2017, p. 121
[37] Bieber, C., 2017, p. 121
[38] Bitecofer, R., 2017, p. 88
[39] Bitecofer, R., 2017, p. 156

4. Conclusion

4.1 Final Answer to Research Questions

After having deeply analyzed the important elements of the presidential election in 2016, I would like to give a final answer to each of my research questions. The first one consisted in how American politics became as polarized as they are today, the second one asks how Trump was able to use this polarization and the last question was in how far Hillary Clinton's nomination was a lucky shot for Trump.

It can be said that Donald Trump was the logical outcome of a development that has been ascertainable since the 1960s. Political polarization rose as a consequence of many factors such as political scandals, preferential treatment of the rich, rising income disparity and the cultural revolution, leading to an alienation from politics as well as a divided political landscape not only within the Senate but also within the American population. During the presidency of Obama, this progress was even more intensified even though he intended to reunite the nation.

Trump was the winner of decades of increasing ideological extremism, laying the foundation for the presidency of a political outsider like him. As Trump pointed out himself, it actually was "a movement, not a campaign", since the reason for his unsuspectedly successful electoral campaign was lesser his own influence and performance than a progress he could not control but was able to take advantage of. He managed to use the growing populist, anti-establishment sentiment for his own sake, utilising nostalgia as a tool to fuel the fear of an internal enemy.

Lastly, it is questionable if Donald Trump's campaign had been as thriving if he had had any other opponent than Hillary Clinton who is (apart from Trump) the most disliked presidential nominee of all times. Clinton was the perfect rival for him since she resembled what (not only) extremist Republicans hated the most: The political elites and the establishment in Washington, an image that haunted her throughout the general election. Another mistake made by the Clinton team was their selective campaign management focusing on swing states and leaving the field to Trump in states considered safe for the Democrats. Finally, a crucial factor leading to Trump's victory was the email-affair in which Hillary Clinton was heavily entangled.

4.2 Prospect: The 2020 Election

Considering all of the scandals Donald Trump has already caused during his first year in office, one could ask themselves if Trump will even stay president until the next election. But – as this research paper illustrates quite impressively – Donald Trump is not like the presidents before him in many respects. Could he maybe be re-elected into office in 2020?

In my opinion it is rather unlikely for Donald Trump to win the election another time. Only one day into his presidency, people started protesting against him (e.g. the "Not My President"-movement) and he received a massive backlash by the media. It is like a countermovement to the one taking place in America in recent years. Maybe Donald Trump is the force uniting a part of the population that is big enough to cause change.

Many Trump supporters have been disappointed by the rate of promises he kept and those he broke. Although Trump stated he was the "president who kept more promises than he previously promised", he actually broke a lot of his election pledges. For example, the wall to Mexico, the ban on Muslims entering the US or the termination of DACA, just to name a few. By now, many voters have realised that Trump might have promised to change the whole system in Washington; in fact, however, he has to yield to the pressure of his fellow politicians just like everyone else.

Furthermore, the three potential Democratic candidates Biden, Sanders and Winfrey all beat Trump in the polls: Biden's result is 17% above Trump, Sanders reached 13% more than Trump and Winfrey gained at least 9% more votes than Trump. Considering that Clinton was a key factor to his success, a convincing opponent could mean the end of the Trump era. However, one has to keep in mind that polls about him were mistaken before and can only be trusted to an extent.

In conclusion, it can be said that there are many arguments opposing a second term of office of Donald J. Trump, such as a huge countermovement gaining ground with each of his controversial actions, his loss of credibility and three promising opponents in the Democratic party. Nevertheless, one has to keep in mind that everything seems to be possible in American politics at the moment and an unforeseen second success could still follow a more than unprecedented first term of office.

5. Sources

5.1 List of References

- Bieber, C., "Nach Obama – Amerika auf der Suche nach den Vereinigten Staaten", 1. Edition, Campus, 2017
- Bitecofer, R., „The Unprecedented 2016 Presidential Election", 1. Edition, Palgrave Macmillan, 2017
- Gellner, W.; Oswald, M., "Die gespaltenen Staaten von Amerika", 1. Edition, Springer VS, 2018
- Johnston, D.," Die Akte Trump", 1. Edition, ecowin, 2016
- Worksheet „Isolationism vs. Internationalism"

5.2 List of Figures

- https://www.google.de/search?q=donald+trump&rlz=1C1VFKB_enDE605DE607&source=lnms&tbm=isch&sa=X&ved=0ah UKEwjZqfrb0dXZAhVKKewKHaD8CkQQ_AUICygC&biw=1366&bih=662#imgrc= 8f-zuagEJfrOuM; 5.3.2018 18:08 [front page]
- https://www.google.de/search?q=donald+trump&rlz=1C1VFKB_enDE605DE607&source=lnms&tbm=isch&sa=X&ved=0ahUKEwjZqfrb0dXZAhVKKewKHaD8CkQQ_AU ICygC&biw=1366&bih=662#imgrc=l1a1bPhNUr2JyM; 5.3.2018, 18:07 [structure]
- Bitecofer, R., „The Unprecedented 2016 Presidential Election", 1. Edition, Palgrave Macmillan, 2017, p. 95 [Fig. 1]
- Bitecofer, R., „The Unprecedented 2016 Presidential Election", 1. Edition, Palgrave Macmillan, 2017, p. 96 [Fig. 2]

5.3 List of Surveys

- CNN Survey „The American Dream is out of reach", 2014
- PEW Research Center Survey „Beyond Distrust: How Americans View Their Government", 2017
- O. Lacewell; S. Regel; A. Volkens: A. Werner, Survey "Manifesto Project"
- Gallup Survey „Trump and Clinton Finish With Historically Poor Images", 2016